Our Lives, Our World

Ireland

Chrysalis Children's Books

First published in the UK in 2005 by
Chrysalis Children's Books
An imprint of Chrysalis Books Group Plc
The Chrysalis Building, Bramley Road
London W10 6SP

Compiled and edited by Susie Brooks
Associate Publisher: Joyce Bentley
Design: Tall Tree Books Ltd
Photographic consultant: Jenny Matthews
Photographic co-ordinator: Peggy Sue Amison
Picture researcher: Miguel Lamas

ISBN 1 84458 443 7

Printed in China

10 9 8 7 6 5 4 3 2 1

British Library Cataloguing in Publication Data for
this book is available from the British Library.

The publishers would like to thank the photographers, Mark
Keegan, Liam Devlin, Grace Donaghue and Sara Greavu, for
capturing the lives of these wonderful children on film. Many
thanks also to Peggy Sue Amison at the Sirius Arts Centre, Cobh,
for all her support and encouragement.

Corbis: Kit Kittle 5(T), Richard T. Nowitz 4(BR); Rex Features:
Mark Campbell 30, Nigel R. Barklie 10(CR); Science Photo
Library: ©GUSTO Front Cover(TR), 1(BC), 5(CR).

Contents

Dia dhuit! – Hello!

We are the children of Ireland and we can't
wait to share our lives with you in this book!

Welcome to Ireland!

We've got so much to show you! Let's start by telling you a bit about our country. We hope you'll come and see Ireland for yourself some time soon!

ATLANTIC OCEAN

Derry (Londonderry)

NORTHERN IRELAND (ULSTER)

Belfast

IRISH SEA

REPUBLIC OF IRELAND (EIRE)

Dublin

Cork

Cobh

CELTIC SEA

Our country

Ireland is an island to the west of Britain in Europe. It is divided into two parts – the Republic of Ireland (called Eire) and Northern Ireland (Ulster). Northern Ireland is ruled by the government in England.

Two capitals

The Republic of Ireland has its own government in its capital city, Dublin (right). The capital of Northern Ireland is Belfast.

4

The Emerald Isle

Ireland is nicknamed 'the Emerald Isle' because it is so green! It is mostly made up of grassy meadows and hills. There are also beautiful mountains, cliffs and beaches.

Our climate

The weather here is mild – summers are cool to warm, and winters are not too cold. Winds bring a lot of rain from the sea, especially to the west of the country. It rains almost every day in many parts of Ireland!

National symbol

Our most famous national symbol is the shamrock.

Our flag

The stripes on the Republic of Ireland's flag relate to our two main religions. Green is for the Roman Catholics, orange is for the Protestants, and white stands for peace between the two.

Speak Irish!

Dia dhuit – hello

slán – goodbye

le do thoil – please

go raibh maith agat – thank you

Claire

Hello! My name is Claire McCartney. I'm 8 years old and I live in Belfast, the capital of Northern Ireland. I have a brother, Evan, who's 2 years old, and a sister called Alex who's 5. Our house has three bedrooms, so Alex and I share.

"My friends think I'm funny, happy and kind. I'm also a little bit cheeky sometimes!"

Here we all are outside our house. We're moving soon, to a house with a garden – it's going to be great! At the moment we go to the park to play. I love kicking a football around with dad.

This is our pet cat, Kitty Cat!

Alex and I both go to the same school. It's a 10-minute walk away. We start at 8.45am and finish at 2.45pm, every day from Monday to Friday. In the mornings we all line up in the playground outside.

These are some of my schoolfriends. We're in Class P5 – there are 26 boys and girls altogether. We all have to wear this green and navy uniform.

Language

Claire says her prayers and takes most of her lessons in Irish. She also learns English and speaks both languages at home. Another word for Irish is Gaelic. About a third of the people in Ireland speak it, while almost everyone speaks English. Most schools teach in English, with Irish as a separate subject. In a few schools, like Claire's, it's the other way round.

Before starting lessons we say prayers in the classroom. Lunch is at 12.00pm. I bring my own sandwiches, crisps, juice and chocolate. I also get fruit, but I don't really like it!

At weekends I like going shopping with mummy. I get £5.00 pocket money every two weeks. I'm buying a party outfit today!

Spending money

Because Northern Ireland is part of the United Kingdom, people use the UK pound (£), called sterling. In the Republic of Ireland people spend euros, as in many other European countries.

pound

euro

This is my local shop. I sometimes pop down here on my own if mummy wants something. They sell all sorts of things, including newspapers, cards and a great choice of sweets.

I go to church on Sundays with my family.

This is me in my First Communion dress. I wore it to a special ceremony when the priest welcomed me to the Catholic Church. I got this certificate, written in Irish.

Religion

Like Claire, most Irish people are Roman Catholics. There are also a small number of Protestants, belonging to the Church of Ireland. All of Ireland's cities have cathedrals, and even a tiny village is likely to have a church.

Eoghan

Hi, my name is Eoghan Neburagho. I'm 6 years old and my home is in Dublin. My parents are divorced and I hardly ever see my dad. But I love living with mum and my big brother Toju. My best friend Craig lives nearby.

Craig

"I'm lovable, lively, curious and kind!"

I'm really close to my mum. She's great at looking after me, and I help her around the house sometimes. Here we are having fun at the local park.

Home!

This is my street – ours is the grey house. We have a small garden at the front and another out the back. I share a bedroom with my mum. Toju has his own room because he's the eldest.

Toju is 23. He manages a sports shop.

Come and have a look around Dublin! To the left is the City Hall, which is full of stories and treasures from Dublin's past.

The old Halfpenny Bridge crosses over the River Liffey.

This is Molly Malone! She was a poor fishmonger who lived in Dublin hundreds of years ago – her ghost is now said to haunt the streets.

Molly Malone

There's a famous song about Molly. It starts like this:

In Dublin's fair city
Where girls are so pretty,
I first set my eyes on sweet
Molly Malone,
As she pushed her
wheelbarrow through streets
broad and narrow,
Crying, "Cockles and mussels,
alive, alive-o".

I live in a part of Dublin called Crumlin. One of my favourite places here is the football pitch! I play for my local team, Crumlin United.

Playing sport

The biggest sport in Ireland is Gaelic football, which is different from ordinary football (soccer). The goalposts are H-shaped and players are allowed to use their hands. Hurling is another traditional sport – it's a bit like hockey but faster. Horseracing, handball, football, rugby and golf are also very popular.

I love going to birthday parties. My friend Ferdia is 7 years old today. He's got two cakes, each with seven candles to blow out!

The party's at the bowling alley. I'm trying to knock down all ten skittles at once!

Halloween is a fun time too. My friends and I dress up to go trick-or-treating. We knock on our neighbours' doors and ask for sweets or a bit of money. If they don't give us anything, we play a trick on them!

I'm the scary skeleton! My friend Oisin (right) is dressed as a vampire with huge fangs.

Look at all my treats!

Halloween

Halloween is celebrated in lots of countries, but many people think it began in Ireland. On the night of 31st October, children dress up as spooks and witches and go from house to house trick-or-treating. Afterwards there are parties with bonfires, fireworks and games. A traditional food is barmbrack – a fruit cake with a lucky ring hidden inside!

Yasmin

Hi! I'm Yasmin Siggins. I'm 8 years old and I live in Cobh, near Cork in the south of Ireland. Our family is quite big – I have four brothers and a sister. We've also got five goldfish and a cat. Dad says when he gets rich he'll buy me a pony!

"Being in this book is the most exciting thing that's ever happened to me!"

Granny
Dad
Mum
Damian
Robert
Khalid
Keanu
Me
Courtney

This is my family. Granny doesn't live with us, but she often visits. Mum mostly looks after us at home while dad goes to work.

We have lots of fun in our house. I love mucking around with my brothers and sisters, but we get told off if we fight too much!

My daddy makes me laugh nearly all the time – except when he's helping with my homework!

This is my town, Cobh. It's built on an island in Cork harbour. I love it because the buildings are all really colourful, and it's by the sea.

"On my birthday I get a day out shopping in Cork!"

We get around town on this bus.

Lots of people like to visit Cobh because it has an interesting past. This is a statue of Annie Moore and her two brothers, who sailed from Cobh to America in 1892.

The signposts that point people around Cobh are written in both English and Irish.

A story to tell

Ireland is popular with tourists because of its beautiful scenery and interesting history. All over the country there are towns, castles and other places with stories to tell. Cobh was the main leaving point for millions of Irish people who fled by ship to America during hard times in the nineteenth century.

The Waterfront at Cobh, County Cork, Ireland

This postcard shows some of the sights in Cobh, including our famous cathedral.

My favourite part of town is the playground. From up on this monkey rope I can see the fishing boats in the harbour!

Life by the sea

Ireland has a very long coastline and lots of rivers, so many people's lifestyles are linked to the water. Sea and river fishing are both common. That means plenty of fish and seafood for people to eat!

This is me and my sister with our friend Claudia who lives by the seaside.

We go to the beach every weekend. I love searching for starfish, mussels and different little fishes. If we catch any, we throw them back in the sea.

There's a tap where we can wash our mucky hands. Keanu and I play a game where we spray each other with water!

"I'd like to go to Spain because it's hot and there are loads of swimming pools. Here it's freezing!"

Declan

Hi, I'm Declan Canning and I'm 8 years old. I live in Derry (some people call it Londonderry) with my mum, dad and two little sisters, Aisling and Svetlana. Our house is a bungalow with a garden out the back.

"I'm not too good and not too bad, but I do like being silly!"

My mum (Janna) comes from Russia – that's why Svetlana has a Russian name.

Aisling and I both have Irish names – dad is Irish. He's called Declan, too!

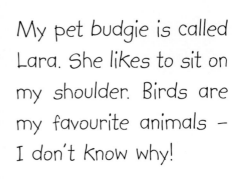

My pet budgie is called Lara. She likes to sit on my shoulder. Birds are my favourite animals – I don't know why!

Every day from Monday to Friday I walk to school with mum.
It takes us 20 minutes. I start at 9.00am and finish at 3.00pm.

My school has 461 pupils. These are some of the boys in my class...

...and these are the girls! We all wear a grey uniform with a stripy tie.

Our teacher is setting us some sums to do for maths. My favourite lessons are English, because it's easy, and science because it's lots of fun!

In art we're making Christmas cards with snowmen on.

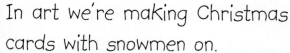

School years

Most children in Ireland start infant school at the age of 4 or 5. Everyone has to go to primary school until they are at least 11, then secondary school until they are at least 15. After that they may choose to leave and find a job, or carry on studying.

"When I grow up I want to be an aeroplane pilot because I'd like to fly up in the sky!"

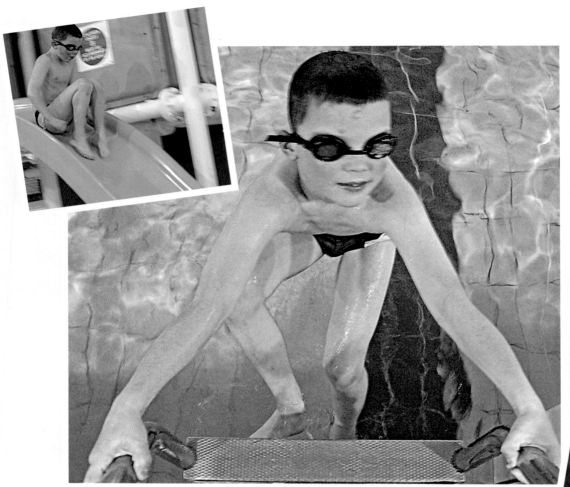

At weekends I like to go swimming at the local pool. Once I got a medal for a race I won! I also love golf and tennis.

My other favourite hobby is playing PlayStation. I'm not allowed to play for more than an hour at a time, but I wish I could stay on it all day!

"One thing I hate doing is reading books."

It's fun messing around in the garden with my best mate Joseph. We hide if mum screams at me to tidy my room – she says it's like a pigsty! But I always come in when she calls me for tea...

Irish cooking

Potatoes are an important crop in Ireland, so most people eat them with their main meals. Champ – mashed potato with spring onions – is a typical dish. Lamb is also widely eaten and is the main ingredient in traditional Irish stew. Fish, cheese, turnips and soda bread are popular too.

Dad's a great cook. Today he's making us Irish stew with champ.

Our Year

JANUARY

New Year's Day In parts of southern Ireland there's a custom called the New Year Swim – people jump into the icy sea for a quick, cold dip!

FEBRUARY

Shrove Tuesday We eat pancakes, to celebrate the day before Lent. During Lent we try to give up something we like for 40 days until Easter.

MARCH

St Patrick's Day The whole country celebrates in memory of our patron saint. On the day, we all wear something green, like a shamrock!

Declan's birthday: 28th March

Spring school holiday: 1 or 2 weeks over Easter

APRIL

Easter We go to church, eat big family meals and exchange chocolate easter eggs!

MAY

May Day Some people still gather flowers such as primroses and dance around decorative maypoles to celebrate the springtime.

JULY

Galway Arts Festival In Galway, in the west, there are two weeks of theatre, dance, music, comedy and other acts from all around the world!

Summer school holiday: 8 weeks from early July

AUGUST

The Puck Fair In Killgorlin (south) there's a crazy street fair with entertainers, fireworks, animal sales and competitions.

Yasmin's birthday: 23rd August

SEPTEMBER

Michaelmas An old Catholic feast day that also marked the end of harvest. Some parts of the country still have Michaelmas markets and many families eat roast goose, the traditional Michaelmas meal.

NOVEMBER

All Saints Day/All Souls Day Religious days when Christians remember and pray for the saints and for the souls of people who have died.

Claire's birthday: 11th November
Eoghan's birthday: 23rd November

DECEMBER

Christmas We put up Christmas trees and decorations, go to church, eat turkey and mince pies, and exchange presents with our families!

Christmas school holiday: 2 weeks in late December/early January

Slán! – Goodbye!

Glossary

barmbrack A traditional Irish fruit cake, eaten on Halloween.

First Communion A holy ceremony that welcomes someone officially to the Roman Catholic religion.

Gaelic Another word for the Irish language.

handball A game in which players hit a ball against a wall with their hands.

hurling A traditional Irish sport played with sticks and a ball, a bit like hockey.

Irish stew A hot-pot made of meat, potatoes and onions.

mussels Shellfish that cling to rocks.

shamrock An Irish plant, like a three-leafed clover.

soda bread Bread made using bicarbonate of soda instead of yeast.

Index